THE MARRIAGE PLAYBOOK™

THE MARRIAGE PLAYBOOK™

Small Group Resource to Help
Build All-Star Marriages

By Ace and Bethany McKay

Sisters, Oregon

THE MARRIAGE PLAYBOOK™
© 2009 by Ace and Bethany McKay

Printed in 2010

All rights reserved. This book or any portion there of may not be reproduced or used in any manner whatsoever without the express written permission of the publisher except for the use of brief quotations in a book review

All contents copyright 2009 by The Marriage Playbook Ministries Inc. All rights reserved. No part of this document or the related files may be reproduced or transmitted in any form, by any means (electronic, photocopying, recording, or otherwise) without the prior written permission of the publisher.

Scripture quotations are taken from the Holy Bible, New Living Translation, copyright 1996, 2004. Used by permission of Tyndale House Publishers, Inc., Wheaton, Illinois 60189. All rights reserved.

Published by
Deep River Books
Sisters, Oregon
http://www.deepriverbooks.com

ISBN 10: 1-935265-26-1
ISBN 13: 9781935265269

Library of Congress: 2010929019

Printed in the USA

Cover design by Joe Bailen

Inside photos courtesy of iStock.com, ClipArt.com and Hermera © 2010, Randy V. Jackson Photography and Victoria Hilyer Photography. All rights reserved.

WHAT PEOPLE ARE SAYING ABOUT THE MARRIAGE PLAYBOOK

I got to meet Ace this year, and what was so cool was his passion for marriage and how God has used his own story to communicate a biblical truth to people about what unconditional love and forgiveness is all about.

—*Stephen Kendrick, pastor, writer, and producer for the movie* Fireproof

The Marriage Playbook is a fantastic idea. At last there's a marriage event that guys can understand! *The Playbook* helps couples formulate a plan in order to deal with the things they'll encounter out on the playing field of matrimony. It does something that hasn't been done in a long time: makes it 'cool' to be married. I'm certain that anyone who participates in a *Marriage Playbook* event will see a profound, positive change in their family life.

—*John Branyan, comedian and author of* Wedlocked

There's no question that marriage is a tough battlefield in today's culture. Many couples are looking for serious help in the midst of the challenges. Enter *The Marriage Playbook*—a dynamic online resource, which provides life-changing tools, counsel, and encouragement that can bring fresh life and hope into any marriage relationship!

*—Bruce Boyd, National Speaker, Family Life
"Weekend to Remember" conferences*

The Marriage Playbook is a forthright fastball of truth for any couple, including my wife and me. Whether a challenge to confront the things we never look at or a solid reminder of the essential tools we, men and women, can so easily forget, *The Marriage Playbook* is the perfect game plan for any marriage.

—Andrew Carlton, Christian recording artist

Like any team, marriages go through season slumps and as a player, I know firsthand that a team can't win unless everyone does their part. *The Marriage Playbook* is *the* perfect tool to coach couples in a way that helps them *win* in their marriage.

*—Will Bartholomew, Former fullback for the
Denver Broncos & President of D1 Sports Fitness*

TABLE OF CONTENTS

Foreword ix
Introduction... xi
1. What Is a Marriage Playbook?........................ 1

Chapters 2 and 3 are designed for individual reading for husbands and wives. After reading separately, come back together to discuss how to apply to your marriage.

2. The Marriage Playbook for Husbands Only 11
3. The Marriage Playbook for Wives Only 21
4. Blending Your New Recruits 29
5. Saving my "Team"................................. 37
6. PSST ... We're talking About Sex.................. 43
Signing Day—Your Team's Contract 51
About The Marriage Playbook 53
About the Author 55

DEDICATION • ACKNOWLEDGMENTS

This workbook is dedicated to: Our Families: Glenn, Kathy, Eric, Denise, Tim "G", Cherry, Justin, Bill, Debbie, Korey, Judy and Mark for being our "12th Man" during our slump season and believing in US even when we didn't. Special thanks to Chris & Judy for an amazing prayer ethic and unconditional friendship for a "Whatever It Takes" attitude. You're right, if you get the Son, You GET IT ALL. A Special, Special shout out goes to our beautiful daughters, Lennon & McCartney. We love you, will always love you, nothing will ever change that and you will always be beautiful. This is also in Remembrance of the biggest sports fan and most colorful person to ever walk life's stadium; Bill "The Birdman" Thomas. You are greatly missed.

FOREWARD

During our experience on season six of the Biggest Loser: Families, Phillip and I realized that if we were going to change our physical bodies we had to have three things to accomplish our goals. First, we had to have a plan or strategy. Secondly, we had to have coaches and a support system to help us implement our plan. Then, finally, we had to put in a lot of hard work to make the plan come to fruition. The result was a weight loss of 256 pounds as a couple! Pretty incredible!

This was not the first time we had to overcome adversity. In 2004, our youngest son, Rhett, was diagnosed with autism, and we lost a business right after we had purchased a foreclosed house that needed over 100,000 dollars of work. So, I found myself living in a construction zone with three small children, one with a disability, and trying to figure out how to find enough money to buy groceries for my family. Needless to say, there was no money to renovate the house and we constantly tried to do everything ourselves, work odd jobs, and take care of our children. I needed to fix my home, I needed to fix my son, I needed to fix my financial situation. Believe me when I say there were days the task of getting out of bed was almost more than I could bear.

One day while I was riding down the road, I was praying and asking God how to fix Rhett. I heard as clear as a bell a voice in my heart saying, "You're not perfect and I love you; why does Rhett have to be perfect for you to love him?" I felt such conviction and at the same time a freedom came over me. I realized it was not my responsibility to "fix" Rhett. He was in God's hands. Before we knew it, we found a therapy that helped Rhett tremendously, got a loan to finish our house, and earned our real estate licenses and became the top agents in our company.

As you can imagine, this period in our lives took a toll on our marriage. We both played the "blame game." We wanted the "better" not the "worse," but here it was and we had to make some choices. We chose to trust God and cling to each other, and eventually we saw the ship start to turn around. After having been married for twenty-one years, we realized the same principles we used to lose weight apply to marriage. As partners you grow and change, life throws you curveballs, and "for better or worse" becomes more than just words you say at the altar. Everyone needs a plan, a support system, and constant effort to keep that commitment as strong as when you said "I do." This is why The Marriage Playbook is such a great tool. It provides the plan and the support system required to help make your marriage the best it can be. It is a constant reminder that marriage is more than just a feeling or a piece of paper; it is a covenant between you, your partner, and God.

Circumstances in life can be overwhelming. Sometimes problems seem too hard to overcome. Life can come at you and make you question your commitments. But with the right plan, coaches, and work, you can accomplish anything you set your heart to!

—Amy Parham

INTRODUCTION

If there's anything I've come to realize in my ministry it is that any time I combine my love for my wife and my love for sports, that's a great day.

During the first year of dating Bethany (my future wife), I had the opportunity to teach her about football. I didn't know then she would one day be my wife, but I knew if she was going to even have a fair shot she had to at least understand my passion for the game. The great thing is my wife now loves the game as much as I do.

I was born a Tennessee Volunteer, and I was raised in the school of Alabama/Auburn rivalries. I even found a few of my own faves along the way as I came to learn the game and find my own passions with what I now truly love about football—with teams like Miami, Florida State, South Carolina, and Syracuse.

The purpose of this workbook is to take sports analogies, particularly the simple methods and practices of football, and apply them to marriage. No tackling, helmets, or shoulder pads required. These simple methods, such as teamwork, playing offense until it's time to play defense, and allowing your marriage to play special teams, will get you in range of your goal—which in football terms means to score a touchdown.

There's nothing in here you can't do, even if you have great, open communication with your spouse. A Marriage Playbook just makes it easier to manage as well as execute. I want you to walk away from this book ready to play for the championship in a Marriage Super Bowl.

At the end of each lesson, as well as at the end of the workbook, there are discussion starters for you and your spouse. These questions don't have to be discussed in a group, only what you feel comfortable with; but you want to make them a priority with your spouse so you get the most from this workbook.

Lastly, there is a commitment card at the end of this workbook that you and your spouse can sign to show your commitment to deepen your vows and help you keep working on a *Marriage Playbook* of your own.

—Ace McKay

CHAPTER ONE

What Is a Marriage Playbook?

The Marriage Playbook is designed to help you create an offensive and a defensive plan for your marriage. It helps you find ways to counteract the opponents that will come at you and your marriage before you ever take the playing field of life together as husband and wife.

You, as husband and wife, are a team. It takes both of you to make your marriage work. Bad habits can form in marriage, but if you establish good habits from the beginning or with a fresh start, your marriage can be a lasting one.

Once a team is put together, no matter the sport, it takes on a new season. This workbook zeroes in on a few areas that can lead to a new level of deeper connection with your spouse:

1. A Good Coach
2. Long-term and Short-term Goals
3. A Playbook
4. Scrimmage Plays

These are essential items without which no team can survive. When you look at what each one of these can do to help a team lay solid building blocks for lots of wins and the hopes of a championship, it's easy to apply the same mindset or game plan to your marriage. You will also look back on "seasons" in life that, although you may seem to have fallen short, you have made great progress from inside the "team."

Here are some questions you can start with as you plan your playbook:
1. What will life be like when we have a baby? Will we both work outside the home? How will a baby affect our finances?
2. What is our budget for the next month? The next year? The next ten years?
3. What would we do if one of us were to die? What if both of us were to die? Who would care for our children?
4. If one of our jobs moves us far from family, how will that affect our marriage and in-law relationships?
5. What part of your past is affecting your marriage?
6. What actions are you taking to change/replace a bad habit with a good one?"

A COACH'S ROLE

A coach is there to draw up a plan for his team. He/She evaluates the needs and plays to each person's strengths. A coach also works to bring out the best in each player. Sometimes it is being an encourager/cheerleader, who allows you to know that "you can do it." A good coach also gives you the truth of any situation. It's never easy to swallow those moments, but you need

WHAT IS A MARRIAGE PLAYBOOK   3

to hear them. This can help you become a better person and be more realistic about what you are trying to accomplish on and off the field of life.

Each person has strengths and struggles as well as needs, goals, and desires. In your marriage, your coaches should be another couple who has played the "game" of marriage successfully long enough to be able to help you learn. They have seen things that work and ones that don't. They can provide perspective and help you see the bigger picture when you are too close to be objective about a decision you are making and how it will affect your marriage. Your coaches can point out the strengths and weaknesses in your "team" and help identify places in your marriage that need addressing. Discuss with your spouse whom each of you can use as a coach in your marriage (a husband for the husband and a wife for the wife).

You could open up a line of communication that makes for a winning team. There's no way for you to know your spouse's needs or vice versa if you don't talk about them. The quarterback talks to the coach, then talks to the players, and has the option

to call an "audible" (to change the play on the fly if he thinks something bad could keep them from accomplishing the goals the next play). The team trusts that something must change to pull off a touchdown. Trusting your spouse is another level of intimacy. Coaching each other can often come across as nagging. Trust has to be earned, but when you talk things out you get on the same page about your life together. You show your spouse you have the best interest for your marriage in your decisions. A coach can pat you on the back when you do something well so you know what good things you can build on.

Now, I do need to point out that trust has to be earned. It's not automatic because you think you deserve it. If you feel that trust is nonexistent in your marriage, then the first step to rebuilding that trust can be to get on your knees and pray about ways to rebuild it. Professional counseling may be something to consider, depending on the state of your relationship. It also will help to get on your knees in front of your spouse and ask him/her to forgive you for tearing that trust down. You can only build trust one day at a time.

People long to be told they are doing well. That is best done through coaching, not critiquing. Being critical in relationships can only build up a wall, not build up your spouse.

If you are a newlywed, you are in the best position to start this so you learn early before you have time to form bad habits. Some of the biggest struggles for coaches are to make players unlearn what they have learned. That sounds very Jedi-like in theory, but it's true. In sports and in marriage, without the proper coaching, bad habits can form quickly.

As the old saying goes, "If you fail to plan, then you will plan to fail." If you don't have a plan in your marriage of what to do when life happens, then you will inevitably fail. No team or solo player ever goes out on the field with the idea to score a goal, make a touchdown, or shoot a basket without a way to achieve it.

Now the question here might be, "I don't know what life's gonna throw at me, so how can I plan?" Well, that's partly true. Based on what happens to other people, you can ask, "What would I do in that situation?" The answers to those types of questions will help you create your playbook.

Are you starting to get the idea? These are some truths in your relationship that if you don't have an offense, you will be forced to play defense. You can't wait for life to happen and just expect to know what to do. When a team goes on the field, court, or rink, the players know what they are going to do to score and score often. When was the last time your marriage scored? You and your spouse have strengths and weaknesses, talents and gifts that, if you learn to play them to your advantage together, you can win one game at a time and eventually win the Marriage Super Bowl.

For starters, pick one place to begin working on, something that can bring you closer and can create oneness. Whatever happens to you happens to both of you.

Praying together is one of the strongest moves you can make on the field. A marriage that revolves around God first is a marriage that can last a lifetime. It's like a team huddle. You talk about what the other needs, you two pray about it, and then you continue to pray about those things when you are apart and together. This opens up so much banter the two of you will never run out of things to say. The first time you huddle there will be things you could share that your spouse never knew was a struggle. A struggle not discussed just builds up walls among the team members and isolation takes over.

You want to just wait till life happens and then see what you're made of? That's why the fifty percent of the marriages that fail FAIL!

Your marriage is a badge of honor. No matter what state it is in. If you have holes to crawl out of, then think of your team as the underdog that is the punch line to every joke. You've probably heard a good joke about the team you hate most. It's funny because it's true. Now the way to make it not funny is to change your team's play and start winning again. This may sound easier said than done, but having an attitude of "whatever it takes" will start you on the road to victory. Whatever needs to happen to change you so *you* can be the best version of *you*.

DESIGNING YOUR PLAYBOOK

If you've ever played a video game system like the Nintendo Wii™ or Xbox, you know there are features on the system or games themselves that allows you to create players. Whether you create your lookalike or a totally different person, it's one of the more popular features of video games these days. It gets even more fun when you get into the team sports games, such as Madden, NCAA College Football, or World Series Baseball—you have the option to create an entire team and/or playbook for your team.

In designing any good playbook, you must have plays of offense that when executed correctly make you score. You also need defensive plays that keep other teams from scoring. Your marriage requires the same thing.

This truth bears repeating: "If you fail to plan then you plan to fail." When it comes to planning your offense or defense for your marriage, you can start with the easy plays you know will occur based on the natural progression of marriage. They are:

1. Children (Are you having any, how many, your time together after the get here?)
2. Sex (Talk it all out—what you like and dislike in the bedroom. It's even okay to pray for you sex life to be the best it can be. When you are married it's not taboo; it can be much better than you can ever imagine.)
3. Money (How to budget it, spend it, save it, and give it away)
4. Jobs/Career (Promotions, relocations, layoffs, stay-at-home moms/dads)

WHAT IS A MARRIAGE PLAYBOOK 7

5. Religion (What church will you attend; how involved will you be?)
6. Outside Relationships (Opposite-sex relationships, guys' and girls' nights, coworker relationships)

Starting with these will open up a great line of communication. Maybe even a fight or two, but you can do this. It's better to know what you're going to do when life happens than not planning and allowing it to bowl you over. Life doesn't stop and wait for you to form a plan. In your marriage, you should be out to win. You're signed up to go all the way to the big game, and the coach is putting you in first string; what are you going to do now? You have to play offense, defense, special teams, and coach. The great thing is you two are a team. Talk every play out as if it were happening tomorrow. That way, when tomorrow comes, you are suited up and ready.

Something else to help you grow closer and find more plays for your playbook is when you watch films or TV shows on relationships, talk about the things that have gone well or failed in your marriage thus far. Hollywood does well at mirroring what's occurring in relationships. Putting yourself in others' shoes can be a playbook builder. When a team wins or loses, a coach goes back and watches film on games they have played to see why something went well or did not. By laying out those plays and tweaking the ones that need practice, you learn to play to each other's strengths. You start to have confidence in your team, that you can do this.

I can't count the number of postgame interviews I've listened to with players who had just lost the game, and they talked about what things they did well in the game and the things they are going to build on for next week's opponent. In your marriage, you're doing the same when you analyze your marriage. We'll talk later about your "12th man" of accountability (see For Husbands and

For Wives sections), but listening to other couples' stories helps your playbook too. Learning from other teams and how well they played together will help you design almost every play possible. These are the people whose life or marriage have been in the dirt and have healed to now help you! You hear how they got through it so that you can be encouraged to do the same.

If you have a 12th man as an individual, choose one the same gender as yourself. Too many times people of the opposite sex comfort each other in times of struggles and find themselves in an emotional or physical affair. Accountability among players, whether your position is wife or husband, is vital to making a marriage work. Couples who have been there and done that need to share their "junk" with other couples, so others can learn the good, bad, and ugly of marriage. You also discover you are not alone and find common ground in your marriage struggles and triumphs.

SCRIMMAGE, SCRIMMAGE, SCRIMMAGE

As you assemble your playbook, the next step is to get into a regular "scrimmage" with your spouse. Teams scrimmage against each other and sometimes against other teams in exhibition to see how their plans and playbook stand up in the heat of the game. So, your next step is to get into good habits that make your marriage (your team) stronger. Some ways to scrimmage are:

1. Pray together and for each other.
2. Date your mate regularly.
3. Spend time with other couples who are real and open about their relationship.
4. Show love daily.
5. When a plan doesn't go right or is abandoned, go back and "watch the film" to learn why.
6. Share your "junk" with other couples. This is not a dump session, especially if your junk is something that involved hurting your spouse. You may want to handle this with

WHAT IS A MARRIAGE PLAYBOOK   9

compassion based on how your spouse will receive your past. There should be caution in how you much you tell all at once. Think of it like a sink of dirty dishes, clean the big pots first.

Planning to play in the Marriage Super Bowl begins by loving your spouse today. Then you wake up tomorrow, and you're doing something that loves your spouse tomorrow. Once you string all those days together, you have a lifetime, and hopefully you have some championship rings to go with it.

SCRIMMAGE STARTERS

1. Why did you get married?
2. What expectations did you have going into your marriage?
3. What is one thing your spouse has done that showed you love?
4. What happened the last time you messed up as it pertains to your marriage/spouse?
5. Talk about your last date night? When's your next one?
6. Out of the five major topics (sex, in-laws, kids, money, jobs), which one(s) do you struggle in?
7. What are you doing to work on these areas?
8. What "snapshot" of you from your past has impacted your marriage the most?
9. What are your expectations of your marriage/spouse now?
10. Do you and your spouse work on money together? Budget? Why or why not?
11. How do you relate spiritually with a spouse who is not as far along in his/her walk with the Lord?
12. What have you learned about God through your marriage?
13. How can you handle situations in your marriage when your spouse thinks you should do something one way and you give your ideas but your spouse takes it as disagreement?

CHAPTER TWO

For Husbands Only

NO APOLOGIES, NO EXCUSES

Let me just be straightforward in saying that the Marriage Playbook was truly written with husbands in mind. If men get passionate about their marriages, our hope is wives will follow. Husbands are naturally set up to be the head of the home, the spiritual leader, and the provider.

HEAD OF THE HOUSEHOLD

I can't help but think of the CBS reality show *Big Brother* when I hear "head of the household." It's a position that's appointed to one person (HOH), with the authority to say what goes into decisions of the house. HOH is also not always liked because of the amount of power that comes from the role. This power often gets abused. For husbands, being HOH can be abused in the same way.

Before we talk about what HOH is, let's talk about what it is not. HOH is not to be bossy, pushy, full of ego, or have the others in the house serve you. This is a fifties' style of thinking. To work as a team in the marriage, you must take your HOH role wisely since you set the tempo for the rest of the house.

Now that HOH has been laid out as to what not to be, what is it exactly? If you are a God-believing person, your HOH position comes from a spiritual nature. See 1 Timothy 3, which mentions being trustworthy, honorable, faithful, gentle, exercising self-control, and managing your children and household well by having a faith in Jesus. HOH should be about setting the bar high for you and your family in all these traits. If you didn't have a good fatherly example growing up, these characteristics may be foreign to you. I grew up with a stepdad, my biological father, my godfather, and my Heavenly Father. It took all these men to shape me. The Bible talks about God being a father to the fatherless (Psalms 68:5). When you need to look to how to be those things as a husband/dad, look to what God expects not what the world expects or dictates.

THE SPIRITUAL LEADER

Evaluate what this means as the spiritual leader in your home. Too many families fall apart because God was not at the center. What does that mean? It means that all decisions, blessings, and trials come from and are a direct result of looking to God for the answers in every situation you or your family face.

When you, as a husband, live out the last part of 1 Timothy 3—to have faith in Jesus—you are humbling yourself to the fact that He rules over your life. He gives and He takes away (Job 1:20–21). In the highest and lowest points of any family, your peace comes from having faith that God has a bigger plan in mind (Jeremiah 29:11). Being a spiritual leader doesn't mean you won't get angry or face real hardships; sometimes it is the complete opposite. However, it can make you a better person simply by trusting that God will guide your words and your actions each day. Life is more than just being a good person.

God can help everyone be better versions of themselves. You have to ask Him to do that. (Note: To have a one-on-one relationship with God is as easy as saying these words, "God I know I have made mistakes, please forgive me and come into my life. Make me a better version of myself. Guide my actions and words to live a godly life.) This is the beginning of a new journey.

THE PROVIDER

By design, a man's nature is to work and provide for his family. Sometimes the wife also works or may be the only one employed. You are still the provider as it pertains to making sure the family is balanced in work and play. You obviously have responsibilities in what your job requires of you, but set your mind to realize that walking away from work at the end of your workday and going home to be with your family is the investment that never depreciates.

Too often, a man allows the bread-winning role to take over his identity as a man. This doesn't define you. No one has ever lived his life and wished he had worked harder at his job. Men usually wish they had been home more and invested in the family. Putting your job before your family, especially ahead of your marriage is dangerous. It's easy to slowly fade into a pattern that often destroys your most important relationships.

God is the ultimate provider. I have a friend who says, "It's all God's Skittles." Recognizing that fact allows you to realize you earn your salary because God knows what you need (see Luke 12:22–24). One way to acknowledge God's ways of providing is to ask Him to help you prioritize your day, to decide when to go home and let the rest of the work/world wait until the next day. This sends a positive message of love to your wife and your family. Being a provider is about providing subsistence, and that means more than just money; it also means time and love.

Men are supposed to do all these things as husbands, yet so many slack on that responsibility. The idea behind *The Marriage Playbook* is to speak "guy talk" to guys about their marriage so they can be the head-leader-provider they were called to be.

So many times "marriage talk" tells husbands to get in touch with their feminine sides so their relationships will be better. Men *don't* have to do that. We are guys and need not apologize for that. I believe if we can just let guys be guys, but speak in a way that inspires, encourages, and also educates, we will all be better husbands and men.

According to the book *Every Man's Marriage: An Every Man's Guide to Winning the Heart of a Woman* by Stephen Arterburn and Fred Stoeker, when women get married they want oneness with their husband. On the flip side of that coin, when men get married they want peace. Women date and search for a man who will take care of them and be compatible with their likes and dislikes, while looking to grow closer/deeper with every day. That doesn't typically go well when all men seek after saying "I do" is peace. Yet, they can go hand in hand—husbands just have to be aware that oneness, like food and clothes, is a necessity for wives. If you want to have peace, you can find it by putting your wife's needs before your own. As you do this out of love and with no thought of what you will get in return, it can radically change your team. Two cool things happen when you put her first:

- She feels loved and wants to show that love back to you by putting your needs ahead of her own.
- The way she puts you ahead of herself is by watching you set the example.

If you and your wife talk about each other's needs and desires together, great. If not, today I dare you to start. I triple-dog-

FOR HUSBANDS ONLY 15

dare you! You'll find love deeper than you ever thought possible. When a team is not on the same page, that's when trading starts to happen among other teams, and that's the one sports reference I hope is not an option. You can do this.

Another dare I want to challenge you with is to start giving first affections to your wife when you come home every day. If you have kids, this shows them the house doesn't revolve around them. They also see that husbands and wives should put each other first (after God) in order for their relationship to last. The cues you took going into our marriages are what you saw or didn't see in your parents' relationship. Those expectations could be holding you back. If your dad came home from work and plopped down on the couch with the remote in hand, you may do the same because you think that's what dads/husbands do. In the meantime, your wife has a different expectation of you when you get home, and being quiet or keeping to yourself is not one of them.

When a team goes on the field/court, they have worked hard every day to achieve oneness as a team. Each player is a limb on an overall body that can only score when everyone is doing his part.

KNOWING YOUR ROLES

The husband's role is first and foremost to love his wife. God says to love her like Jesus loved the church. Now, to love your wife unconditionally takes on different layers of love. The kind of love you have for your team(s) is also a good example of unconditional love. No matter whether they win or lose, they are "your" team and your devotion is there in the tough times as well as at the championships. No one can talk bad about your team, right? You love to say this is a rebuilding year when things don't go as hoped this season. If you are in a rebuilding year, today is the day that rebuilding begins to take shape.

Let's unveil a myth. Love is not that feeling you had when you first married. Love is not a feeling at all; actually, it's a choice to be there for your wife until "death do you part." Love is difficult because on your wedding day you can't begin to imagine what the bad stuff will be when you commit to "for better or worse." In order to love her correctly, you must show her love. She has to see your actions matching your words. She has to see it in your eyes as well as your heart. You're playing to win, not to not lose.

By waking up each morning and choosing to love your wife, you are also saying you desire her, you show devotion to her, and that includes being tender to her. I hope wives will learn to tell their husbands about the ways men can be tender, because this doesn't come natural to them and it's different for each woman. You are learning to lead your heart, not follow it.

Also, being attracted to her, devoted to her, and seeing her as a gift are other ways to love her. If your actions come from these things, you will find passion for your marriage. Today is a good day to go back and start planning for the events in life that beat up on couples and marriages. Your wife will take cues from you on starting your playbook, so let's wow them in our actions.

Taking the time to learn how to speak all five love languages Dr. Gary Chapman explains in his book *The Five Love Languages* will prove to be a key to a successful playbook. Your wife has one or two ways that speak love to her the best. You should know this as well as a quarterback knows the plays that make his team look the best on game day. However, don't neglect the love languages that seem less important to her because, when those go unspoken for a while, they can quickly become a primary need or desire she may try to fill other ways or with other people when they are not shown at home.

The five love languages are:
1. Physical Touch (doesn't always mean sex)
2. Words of Affirmation (can be spoken, a simple love note, or a text message)

FOR HUSBANDS ONLY   17

3. Acts of Service (doing something she knows needs done but doesn't have time for, as well as the things she leans on you for on a regular basis—especially without being asked)
4. Gifts (don't have to be expensive)
5. Quality Time (Date nights need to be a regular occurrence. Babysitters are an investment in your relationship. Even swapping kids with other couples—you can easily set another couple to be accountable for dates without the added cost)

If don't know your wife's main love language, just watch how she shows love to you the most. That's a good tip about how she wants to receive love from you. Talk together about how you each perceive love.

YOUR 12TH MAN

Like any good team, a 12th man can help you win games. My wife and I have been to many Southeastern Conference games and have heard the roar of the fans that helped their team stop the opponent from scoring or helped their team rally back from behind. A Marriage Playbook needs a defense and a 12th man (someone to cheer you on and motivate you to do your best). What this will do for you as a man is find accountability on how to love your wife and how to keep outside defenses from coming at you, i.e. other women, daily stress, etc. The 12th man can cheer you on when you need it. You are not alone in the things that happen to you. Who in your life now can be your 12th man?

When you have found someone to be your 12th man of accountability, listening to his stories helps your playbook too. Learning from other teams and how well they played together will help you design almost every play possible. You really start to put yourself in others' shoes by asking, "What would I do in that situation?"

These are the people whose life or marriage have been in the dirt and have healed to now help you! You hear how they got through it so that you can be encouraged to do the same. If you have a 12th man as an individual, choose one the same gender as yourself. Too many times, as mentioned in the previous chapter, when people of the opposite sex comfort each other in times of struggles they find themselves becoming involved in an emotional or physical affair. Accountability among players is vital to making a marriage work. Those couples who have been there and done that need to share their "junk" with other couples, so others can learn the good, bad, and ugly of marriage. You also discover you are not alone and find common ground in your marriage struggles and triumphs. When a man shares struggles with a woman it is like playing with fire, and you will get burned.

As you talk with your 12th man, use this time to open up about sex. Guys talk about it in ways that seems like bragging most days. Remember, this is your wife. You should be discreet, especially since your 12th man may know your wife; but the conversations should be honest so that you can talk about your struggles with temptations. It doesn't take long for online sites, magazines, movies, or even other women around you to slowly lead to behavior harmful to your marriage. The 12th man can only help you in this area if you are open and honest with him.

A 12th man should take on the same vow of silence a doctor would to his patient—no one is to know what you talk about when you hang out. A simple breech, even to your own wife, can build up walls, and then you will have isolated the very reason you have accountability anyway.

Being honest with your 12th man about everything starts with being honest with yourself, having accountability within your own mind and heart.

BENCH NOTE

Guys, I'm benching you for a second to say that the reason these things are important is because I failed them for a time in my marriage. I allowed my job, my personal goals, and my lack of focus on what is truly important in this world to cause me to make mistakes ... I shut down communication with my wife. I allowed her mood to dictate my mood, and from there it spiraled into two affairs before I destroyed every level of intimacy in my marriage. I lost her trust but never her love. It was her choice to wake up and pray for me every day. My challenge to you is to take pride in your marriage. God gave you a beautiful woman for a reason, and together you can find love that's worth fighting for. We don't have to let the mistakes of our past keep us from the joys in this world. Our record, even if you are 0-fer, doesn't have to define the rest of the season. We learn from broken tackles and missed layups so that we can improve and not be doomed to repeat our bad behavior.

HOMEWORK:

You will become a self-proclaimed expert by being a student of your wife. I have a few books that have helped in my search to be a better man and husband. Here are some books to encourage your inner best:

The Power of the Praying Husband by Stormie Omartian

Every Man's Battle: Winning the War on Sexual Temptation One Victory at a Time by Stephen Arterburn and Fred Stoeker

Every Man's Marriage by Stephen Arterburn, Fred Stoeker, and Mike Yorkey

For Men Only by Shaunti and Jeff Feldhahn

CHAPTER THREE

For Wives Only

Okay, wives, if you have gotten this far, you are probably wondering: *Why all the sports analogies?* Well, there are hundreds of marriage help Web sites, books, and ministries that lean toward the female side of marriage. They focus on getting men to talk about their feelings and being romantic and all that mushy love stuff chick flicks are written about every day. These resources may give your marriage a boost for a short time, but they often just do not speak to men.

The men are supposed to be the spiritual leaders of the household, and all too often they are asked to be more sensitive and get in touch with their feminine side. These resources may work, but really how much of that stuff gets through to a guy? Our resources use sports analogies to help men feel more connected to what is being presented. They also won't be so far out there that you have to know something about sports or that a guy who doesn't will be lost. I (Bethany) am a woman who loves football. My husband says I can carry my own in a conversation with any man when it comes to college football, but start talking about basketball or hockey and my eyes glaze over. *The Marriage Playbook*, while using sports analogies, will also explain things so a woman can get as much from it as a man.

When it comes to marriage, women are usually all too eager to go to a conference, read a book, or talk about it with other women. Men, on the other hand, tend to go along because their wives want them to, and that is not what women really want. Women should want to be their husbands' cheerleader not their coach. Wives want men to be pumped up about their marriage like they get pumped up for Saturday's big game. What woman wouldn't want that?

THE TEAM

I don't know how much you know about a team, but if you have ever watched any sport, even little league, you know the best teams are the ones who work together. The same thing holds true for marriage. You and your husband are a team. You work best when you work as a team and tend to have problems when one or both of you stop trying to function as a team. This isn't to say that you do everything together. Just like a team, every player has a position to play. A baseball team wouldn't work if everyone wanted to be the pitcher. Your marriage won't work if you both try to fill the same role. That includes having an identity outside of your role as wife. Sure, you need to discuss important decisions like major purchases, moves, and children, but the role you each play on the overall team isn't going to be the same. You still need to work as a team, however, if you want to have an All-Star Marriage.

OUR ROLES

Your idea of the husband's and the wife's roles in a marriage was probably created while you were growing up watching your parents. Did Mom do all the housework? Or was it a group effort? Did both parents work outside the home, or was your mom a stay-at-home mom? Were you raised by a single parent? All of what you observed built your idea of the roles husbands and wives play. Your husband also saw how the roles functioned in his family, and he has his own ideas. Very rarely are both partners' the same, so you probably spent the first year or more of your marriage playing out the same roles you saw in your own home growing up. I have always been the one to do laundry in my home. Not because I thought it was woman's work; in fact my dad did laundry in my home. I chose that role early in our marriage. My husband balances the checkbook because early in our marriage, he took on that role when he realized I had never done it in my entire life. For you, it may be completely opposite, but you have slowly fallen into your individual roles.

Have you thought about what your main roles in your marriage are? I honestly never had until listening to a friend talk about it one day during a hard time in my marriage. The husband's role in marriage is to love his wife (Ephesians 5:33). The wife's role, however, is to respect her husband. Sounds crazy, right? Actually, wives are to love their husbands, but being women that comes naturally for us. Women are programmed to love; that's why in a lot of cases the woman will fall in love with a guy she is dating long before he falls in love with her. Granted, she may not tell him before he tells her, but more often than not she falls first. It is just how woman are wired. Men, on the other hand, are built to desire respect. They don't want to be put down or made to feel like what they do isn't important, so, for them, respect is what they are looking for from women.

What exactly does respect look like? Well, it isn't treating him like one of the kids and telling him what to do or complaining about the way things are. Respect is showing your husband that what he does is important to your family. Many women fall into the trap of complaining about not having enough money or the long hours he works. What women think they are saying is, "You work so hard, I think you deserve more than you make." What men hear is, "You aren't a good provider, and you're never home." Taking the time to explain this or reword it in the first place can make a world of difference in his perception of feeling your respect for him.

Saying something like, "Honey, I know you are working hard and I appreciate how hard you work for our family, but when you work long hours I miss you and I wish you could be home more." Presenting the thought this way you can discuss it without it sounding like nagging but rather as a "Here's something I am feeling or thinking; what's your thought on it?" and tends to help the words come across as respectful as well.

BEING YOUR HUSBAND'S CHEERLEADER

Whether you were a cheerleader in school or not, it may drag up positive or negative images in your mind. Ultimately, you cheer for things about which you are a fan. Being a fan of your husband automatically should make you his cheerleader.

Your husband wants to feel supported. God designed him with a need to be the provider; unfortunately, not all men do well at this. Even if the wife works, the weight of feeling like he is taking care of his family rests on the husband's shoulders. So encourage him. Thanking him for what he does as a provider, no matter how big or small, can encourage him to step up his game. When he tells you about something good that happened at work, show him you care. Cheer him on if he goes for a promotion or new job.

Just like cheerleaders on the sidelines understand the game they are cheering for, a wife needs to understand the job her husband does. This does not mean being able to do his job if he were to suddenly become incapacitated, but learn enough about it so that when he tells you about his day it makes sense to you and you know what to be enthusiastic about. It is also helpful when you get together with people from his work so you know what they are talking about.

Another, way to be his cheerleader is to be excited when he arrives home. Think about football games when the team comes running onto the field. The cheerleaders are cheering and dancing because they are excited about their team. Now, you don't have to put on a costume and be standing there shaking pompoms as he walks in the door, but greet him at the door. You get the first kiss. Drop what you are doing and let him know you are happy to see him. This is important for your children to see as well because it lets them know your husband comes first. All too often these days we let the kids think the world revolves around them and their wants and needs. When they get into the real world, they will realize it doesn't. You are doing them a disservice if they think they are more important than your marriage.

Cheerleaders also are there to help cheer the team on when it is not doing so well, to pump the players up to come back and rally to win. As your husband's cheerleader, it is your job to cheer him on and encourage him. If he didn't get a promotion or a child is sick, etc., that can be a "losing streak" in your marriage. Serving as your team's cheerleader can make all the difference when your team is behind.

THE 12TH MAN

In football, each team has eleven men on the field during each play, but you will often hear announcers talk about the 12th man. Actually, if there is a 12th man on the field, the team gets penalized, but most of the time when they talk about the 12th man they mean the fans. The crowd cheers louder when the other team is trying to score. They also cheer for their team when they do something well or when they are trying to rally the team for a comeback; the same goes for marriage. Your 12th man is someone outside your marriage who has more experience and wisdom. A mentor couple who has seen their team through hard times makes a great "12th man," or each spouse can find a 12th man in someone of the same sex to talk with who can cheer them on. The 12th man always needs to be someone of the same gender. Wives need to talk to other wives, and husbands need to talk to other husbands. Otherwise, your 12th man could end up on the field and you could get penalized in the form of a physical or emotional affair.

When you talk to your 12th man about your marriage, be honest with her. She can't help you if you don't tell the truth. This is not the time to sit around and complain about your husband—that wouldn't be showing respect—but rather talk about your troubles is a discreet way that doesn't make her lose respect for him as a man. You wouldn't want your husband complaining about you, so show him that same respect. Remember you're his cheerleader. When women get together it is very easy for them to complain about their husbands' flaws, but if you want to have a strong team you can't badmouth your teammate. When quarterbacks badmouth another player on their team during an after-game interview this only adds tension between them and doesn't motivate them to play better in the next game.

YOUR PLAYBOOK

In all sports, each team has a playbook. These playbooks have plays designed to help them score and to get them out of bad situations, along with special plays and defensive plays. It is the job of each player to know those plays backward and forward so all the coach has to do is say a number or give a hand signal and the players know what to do.

Your team needs a playbook too; this is where the talking part that the women like comes in. When we get married we say "for better or worse." Most people can't even imagine what the worse could be, but that worse will come, and if you aren't prepared for it then your team won't know the play to pull out. In sports, teams watch films of other teams playing and see where their weaknesses are and what they tend to do in a crisis. You and your husband can do that too. You have seen couples who have had some kind of marriage or family crisis, but have you talked with your husband about what you would do in a similar situation?

Even if it is just in a movie you are watching, you can use that as a time to add to your playbook. Discuss it with your husband. Plan moves ahead of time to avoid a bad situation, such as promise not to be alone with someone of the opposite sex for any reason. Also, talk about how you would handle it if a crisis did happen to you. What would you do if one of you lost your job? What would you do if one of you or your children became seriously ill? How far would you be willing to move for a new job? There are hundreds of questions you could come up with. While you can't plan for everything, if you have discussed it beforehand, it will be easier to deal with it if/when it comes along. Remember, if you fail to plan then you plan to fail. Don't let your team fail.

HOMEWORK

Here are a few books to help you become a better woman and wife:

The Power of a Praying Wife and *The Power of a Praying Woman* by Stormie Omartian

Beautiful in God's Eyes by Elizabeth George

The Excellent Wife: A Biblical Perspective by Martha Peace

For Women Only by Shaunti Feldhahn

FOR HUSBANDS AND WIVES
SCRIMMAGE STARTERS

1. Who have your found, or who will you find, to be your 12th man?
2. (Husbands) What are you doing to show love to your wife?
3. (Wives) How are you being a cheerleader for your husband?
4. What is your spouse's primary love language? What are you doing to "speak" it?

Blending Your New Recruits

As each season of any professional sport winds down, a session of trading begins among the teams. It may be money, less than stellar stats from the previous season, or age or bad attitude that gets a player cut or traded to another team. My favorite on the list of reasons to trade a player is that they simply don't fit the team. Sometimes a coach or team needs a new direction, and a certain player's talents don't fit that new direction.

In marriage and family relationships people often think the trading aspects work about the same. There might come a time when the reality of a marriage/family splitting up happens. However, this does not mean if you find your marriage in trouble that trading is the only option. It is NOT! It takes work, but your marriage can improve. Extreme methods may be required, such as counseling, weekend retreats, etc., before you see results in your relationship. But, just like a team is committed to an attitude of "whatever it takes" mentality to win in a game when they are behind or to turn the 0–6 season into a playoff spot, your attitude is the beginning of getting back on track.

You may have heard the saying "winners never quit," and it applies to marriage too. In counseling, couples in their second or third marriage have the hindsight to realize that being married to someone new did not change the problems in marriage. Your struggles are common; however, they don't have to be a struggle when you have the attitude that quitting is not an option.

If a divorce and remarriage has occurred, a new dynamic emerges that you have to make work among not just husband and wife but with children and ex-spouses too. Especially when children are involved, there is a high level of priority to get your team on the same page. Since trading in blended families can't occur like it does in sports, the main focus of this section is to look at your team now as if you have new recruits, and use the talents of each player to strengthen your new team.

While sixty-five percent of remarriages involve children from a previous marriage to form a blended family, the new family unit often does not mesh well. In reality, depending on the children's ages at the time of remarriage, common family blunders can cause elevated levels of tension a nuclear family may not have to deal with.

For instance, when a parent helps or spends more time with a stepchild than a birth-child, resentment may settle in at a higher level than among birthright siblings. Jealousy can build thick walls in any family; however, coming from a blended family myself and watching couples struggle to make their new recruits work together well, I've seen that jealousy festers into anger. It could be due to the "his kids/her kids" issues of blended families. This concept derives from the idea that blended-family children sometimes believe their family is always two halves that happen to function under one roof. They may share a house and what's in it, but the relationship is still very much divided.

When this complexity occurs, it can put parents in a situation where they feel forced to choose sides. The parents don't mean to do so, but it's emotionally and physically natural to gravitate toward their biological children. Be aware of this inclination and step back from any such scenario to determine if this is happening.

Another tension point of this complexity comes from the kids. The anger/sadness they may still harbor from the mom/dad who left their original family is now being projected toward the new stepmom/stepdad of the blended family. If your children are doing this, don't dismiss the importance of these emotions. They need to deal with them in a healthy way. Professional counseling may be needed to assist with this process.

Three resources in your home can help better blend your team. Before we touch on these, I want to bring up a very important factor to get into as a family before you start to move forward from today. When couples get married, whether for the first time or a remarriage, certain expectations come into that marriage. It could be expectations of what they saw or didn't see from their own parents as husband and wife or from a former spouse. There is also the level of self-identity couples look for so they can have a strong, romantic, love-filled life as husband and wife. Couples *have* to talk these things out.

Our *Start Smart* resource at *The Marriage Playbook* Web site can help identify issues where you still need to become more likeminded, even if you're not a newlywed. When if comes to blended families, the same rules apply; there are expectations between the couple as well as among the children. All the ideas, what-ifs, and doubts need to be addressed so everyone is on the same page. If there's a level of unspoken expectation in a child's mind as to how the new family will work and it is not met, a breakdown in communication begins.

When I was growing up, my parents would often call family meetings to talk about an issue of struggle. By the end of the meeting we all understood how things would work for that particular problem. It didn't mean Mom or Dad dictated the solution. My brother and I would have input as well. It also didn't mean we never yelled. Those moments occur. Respectfully hearing all sides and then discussing the best options can help the resolution come more smoothly. Every member of the family should have a say, but the parents hold veto power. Finding ways to keep those lines of communication open will help the blending process.

Now, back to using the very resources you already have in order to improve the relationships in your blended family (or any family, for that matter).

1. THE CONCESSION STAND

The concession stand, also known as the kitchen table, is not just for meals. It's good for sitting together for homework, playing games, etc. The reason for the importance of the kitchen table for helping bring families together is similar to when two people meet at a restaurant. No matter how long you've known the person, there is something about sharing a meal or coffee that helps people relax and talk about what's going on in their lives.

The open banter at home is necessary for kids because they need a safe place to talk freely about subjects and issues and not be judged. These are the topics you don't want them going to uninformed friends, neighbors, or relatives about. The kitchen table can become that centerpiece in the house catching the crumbs, the tears, and the laughs your family will share together.

2. FINDING A BLENDED 12TH MAN

The one point really unique in *The Marriage Playbook* is the importance of having a 12th man in marriage. To remind you, in football, each team has eleven men on the field during each play, but you will often hear announcers talk about the 12th man. Most of the time when they talk about the 12th man, they refer to the crowd. The fans cheer for their team when they do something well or when trying to rally the team for a comeback—the same goes for marriage. Your 12th man is someone outside your marriage who has more experience; your 12th man is the accountability you need to make your marriage stronger.

In blended families, the 12th man is other blended families. You can learn a lot from those who have gone through the same issues you are or will be facing. You're not alone in these struggles, so stop pretending you are. If you don't believe me, find some blended families and get to know them.

These first two resources tie together well in that when your kids won't come to you, they may feel more comfortable opening up to someone from the other blended family. If you choose your 12th man wisely and find ones who are likeminded, you can feel safe that the advice they share with your children is the same as if they were their own.

3. LOOK AT THE MANUAL

Finally, and most importantly, faith in God and his reasons for bringing your family together can shape your blended relationships in an amazing way. The Manual, a.k.a. the Bible, is our guideline for any challenges in the midst of blending two families. Jesus Himself was from a blended family (since Joseph was not his physical father) so He understands the struggles that come with blended families.

Jeremiah 29:11 sums this up nicely. God says: "For I know the plans I have for you … plans for good and not for disaster, to give you a future and a hope."

When your children and spouse see you reading the Bible and praying, it offers them a powerful symbol of hope. As they observe change in you over time, they will see why and where it comes from. First Timothy Chapter 3 is one passage that offers great rules for your home, even if you don't believe in God.

> This is a trustworthy saying: "If someone aspires to be an elder, he desires an honorable position." ... an elder must be a man whose life is above reproach. He must be faithful to his wife. He must exercise self-control, live wisely, and have a good reputation. He must enjoy having guests in his home, and he must be able to teach. He must not be a heavy drinker or be violent. He must be gentle, not quarrelsome, and not love money. He must manage his own family well, having children who respect and obey him. ...
>
> In the same way, deacons must be well respected and have integrity. ... They must be committed to the mystery of the faith now revealed and must live with a clear conscience. Before they are appointed as deacons, let them be closely examined. If they pass the test, then let them serve as deacons.
>
> In the same way, their wives must be respected and must not slander others. They must exercise self-control and be faithful in everything they do.
>
> A deacon must be faithful to his wife, and he must manage his children and household well. (1 Timothy 3:1-4, 8-12)

If you've never prayed with your family before, don't get hung up on words, just speak out loud the same type of words you use to talk to your spouse—respectfully, passionately, and with a desire to listen.

As you implement these resources, let me say, I've found doing them in reverse order works best. It sets a new dynamic in your family. Establishing God's word as the foundation for any relationship will always make it stronger.

BLENDING YOUR NEW RECRUITS 35

SCRIMMAGE STARTERS

1. What expectations did you have when blending your family?
2. What expectations did your children have?
3. What conflicts tend to arrise often?
4. Were your expectations realistic? Why or Why Not?
5. What's working well in your blended family?
6. What have you learned from other blended families?
7. Do you find it hard bonding with your new children? What are you doing to develop that relationship?

CHAPTER FIVE

My Team Needs Saving

God hates divorce. However, He allows it to happen sometimes so His grander scheme can play out.

I'm a firm believer that if a marriage can be saved, it should be. Not only because of your vows on your wedding day or even the biblical principle behind why God wants us to stay together. It should be saved because of the emotional rollercoaster you have to ride in order to get to the other side if you separate. The grass isn't greener on the other side; it's only greener where you water it.

I love the analogy in the movie *Fireproof* when Caleb Holt is talking to his best friend, Michael, about the condition of his marriage. Michael takes salt and pepper shakers and superglues them together to represent the bond between a husband and wife. As Caleb goes to pull them apart, Michael stops him by saying, "Don't do it, you'll end up breaking one if not both of them." That's what happens when a marriage ends—it simply breaks you.

If your marriage is in the "slumps" or your spouse won't budge to make it work, realize that more times than none, one half of the team wants out and you can't do much, if anything, about it.

When Manny Ramirez made it vocal that he wanted to leave the World-Series-champion Boston Red Sox, they did all they could to change his mind and heart to stay. After all the talks, Ramirez ended up leaving and became a Los Angeles Dodger. His heart wasn't in it, and the Sox knew that if he stayed he wouldn't be playing his best for the team. Winning is harder to do when the whole team is not on the same page. The sad truth for many marriages is that they won't make it on the same team their whole life. The good news is that from the heartache of divorce can come reconciliation, healing, and an unbelievable amount of strength.

Now, here are a few things to check to make sure you are doing all you can to make your marriage work. Even right up to the day divorce papers are final, these are things that might help you or at least give you a peace of mind for what's to come.

1. "WHATEVER"

Saying "whatever" means you are willing to do whatever it takes to bring you and your spouse into good standing with God. You make choices everyday that affect your marriage positively or negatively, and when you make enough bad choices, the sacrifice of losing that relationship may be what God has in store in order to bring you or your spouse closer to Him.

We can't change our spouses, only God can do that. Praying "whatever" says you're asking that whatever needs to come to light will. It also means whatever needs to happen to bring your spouse to his or her knees. It doesn't mean whatever it takes to fix your marriage. Whatever means *whatever* God wants. He is the only one who sees the big picture. What we think needs to happen and what God sees needs to happen are not always the same thing.

2. TEAM SUPPORT

Are you doing all you can to show love to your spouse? That may be forgiving them for something they have done to hurt you. It could be changing your schedule to be more available at home. This is another part of whatever. Whatever applies to taking the action of allowing God to change you. It can help your faith grow so that if your marriage does end, you can have a peace knowing you are being obedient to God.

3. COMMUNICATE YOUR PASSION FOR THE TEAM

If you haven't already, go on record with your spouse that you don't want a divorce—not in a harsh way, but still showing passion and belief for your marriage. I remember when my wife and I had just returned from a meeting with an attorney, she looked at me and told me she thought the divorce was stupid. Not that I was stupid, but I was so far gone in my marriage I truly wanted out.

As you pray "whatever," ask God to reveal the things you need to know to show true love to your spouse. When God has defined that for you, expressing it to your spouse can have a positive affect. Your spouse needs to know that the patterns you once had will be changing. Your actions show an obedience that wasn't there before and, by that example, you show leadership of how faith plays into your life. My wife was my prayer champion through the darkest times in our marriage. She will be the first to tell you that even though the "whatever" prayer was the hardest thing to pray, knowing she didn't want out of the marriage, she never stopped praying and hoping.

The truth for crisis in marriage is you never wake up and find your marriage in trouble; it's a slow fade. Bad habits gradually develop, like not communicating, not showing affection, or not putting your spouse's needs before your own. You slowly fall into those routines, and over time your marriage goes into a slump.

The odds are stacked against you from the moment you say, "I do." One-half of married couples don't make it. Marriage requires work and open communication. A focus on God at the center of your lives gives you a better chance of survival. If your marriage is not or has never been built on a foundation of faith, God may allow for it to dissolve so that He can place you in a better environment, married or single.

4. FORGIVE YOUR TEAMMATE

There's a cycle that goes on when you've been wronged by your spouse. You're angry, then sad, then angry some more, then disappointed, then *really* angry, then confused, and, hopefully, eventually forgive. Let me say this, the anger is normal and you have every right to be angry. To dismiss the emotions someone feels when they have been betrayed only draws out the forgiveness process. As someone who has had to seek forgiveness for some stupid things in my life, I've learned firsthand that you have to start by forgiving yourself. You can't walk around and allow your guilt for your past to define who you are now. You can and maybe already have made changes from how you used to be. That was just a snapshot of your former self. It's a picture you may not want people to see of you, but it's in the past.

The Bible says in Matthew 6:14–15: "If you forgive those who sin against you, your heavenly Father will forgive you. But if you refuse to forgive others, your Father will not forgive your sins."

So with that truth spoken, learn to let go of what has been done to you. Things happen to you just for you. They happen so you can help other people who may go through similar situations.

Also, when you forgive your spouse, you are not saying what they did was okay. What you are saying is that you're letting it go and will never pick it up again because you can't live with that kind of anger for the rest of your life.

Now you might be the one who needs to seek forgiveness. The humility and transformation that needs to occur is not an easy process. As you learn to lean on God, maybe for the first time, you will see how He can change your heart. You will start to find the words that begin that healing with your heart. When the words are hard to find but your heart is in the right place, talk out with your spouse what levels of commitment you are going to take to can keep you from going down this road again because it will only lead to more hurting. A great song that expresses what you need to convey to seek forgiveness is Hoobastank's "The Reason." (You can find the words online.)

Fixing a marriage is difficult. A marriage breakup is even harder, and the things in life that are worth fighting for should be. Even with those truths, God still allows things He hates to happen so He can accomplish His purposes. It's never easy on either side of the coin, but focusing on Him and allowing Him work in your life can build you up better than we were before.

SCRIMMAGE STARTERS

1. What do you need to forgive your spouse for? (Big or little things)
2. What do you need to seek forgiveness for? (Big or little things)
3. If you are on the fence, and divorce seems to be the direction you are headed, which of these points is hardest?
4. What are you *now* doing to show love through the crisis?

Psst...We're Talking About Sex

The million-dollar question we get asked by married couples the most is: How do you keep sex amazing in your marriage?

Before that can be answered, a main communication breakdown in the bedroom must be removed. Real sex is not like it is in the movies. Hollywood has managed to put sex on a pedestal and makes people think it's like Patrick Swayze in *Roadhouse*, where it's against a wall, with no need for a towel afterward. Whatever!

It can be hot. It can be sweaty. It can even be against the wall. The main link for sex to be exciting and stay that way is to simply talk. Communication is key to marriage and essential for a great sex life.

For your sex life to be amazing in your marriage, telling your spouse what you like is imperative. Also, share what you dislike. How else are you going to know and to meet each other's expectations? It's a good lesson for other areas too. You'll soon learn that the more you talk about your desires in the bedroom, the more you discover you are on the same page in every moment of your lives together, and the better your marriage can be.

Another helpful tip is to pray for God to make it amazing. There is a reason to scream out God's name in the middle of sex—it's praise to the Creator during the best moment of intimacy between a husband and wife.

In order to open up these doors of sexual freedom with your spouse, there are a few barriers that have become the "elephant in the room," which need to come out of the darkness so they no longer define your sex life and hold you back.

BARRIER #1: It's taboo before you get married, and after the wedding it's suddenly okay.

Part of what makes sex exciting when premarital sex occurs is that, because of being bad by doing it outside of marriage, it has an elevated excitement you lose after marriage. That's why waiting till you are married is important because then you don't associate that emotion with sex once you say, "I do." It can be exciting for the right reasons.

The reality is that most people don't wait, so you have to train your mind and heart to let go of those feelings that sex is still bad or it should always feel like it did before marriage. If this is you, take peace in knowing that God created sex for a husband and wife to enjoy (see 1 Corinthians 7). The point in which you let this barrier down and push away the images you may have from previous experiences, the more intimate you will become with your spouse as you go through this part of the journey together.

BARRIER #2: I'm afraid of what my spouse will think if I suggest _____.

As you discuss the positions and touches you enjoy from your spouse, don't be afraid to be honestly raw. A major point that cripples married couples from sharing is they are afraid of what their spouses will think. If your spouse tells you something he or she wants, and you are uncomfortable with that, being honest about it will at least help you set up the boundaries with the bedroom. Talk about it in a loving, nonjudgmental manner.

BARRIER #3: I don't believe it can be better.

If you've been in a situation your whole marriage, maybe longer, where sex has been a weapon or misused, it may be difficult for you to really enjoy it. People who have been molested, raped, or taken advantage of in any way sexually often see sex as more of a service or something that is very painful. Sex can be beautiful and pleasurable, but a few things have to happen first. You will need to be open with your spouse about what you've been through. As the spouse on the receiving side of this information, you can help find your spouse's pleasure areas. This will take time, but the patience and investment will bring your intimacy level up. Work to make it enjoyable for both partners.

BARRIER #4: I believe in Hollywood's version of sex.

Movies and TV shows give unrealistic expectations of most relationships. It's not just in the feelings of love or following your heart or a romantic story that always has you kissing or lovemaking on the beach in the rain. That's not how life is. Love is a choice, and you have to lead your heart in your marriage for it to truly work. When you follow your heart or look for the feelings or the hot sex that may have existed in the early years of marriage, you are fooling yourself. Those sappy kind of feelings and love eventually fade, but if the proper foundation of intimacy and open communication stay open, you will grow deeper in love in your marriage. This can help lead to great non-Hollywood sex. You'll find it even improves with age.

BARRIER #5: I never had it good.

No matter what your experience of sex is or how long you have been married, there are expectations in your mind and often ones that remain unspoken. This goes beyond the bedroom, but also includes it. In not talking about what you want in the sexual area of your marriage, you may find you have never experienced sex at its best. Since most people don't talk about sex unless they are bragging, something you never want to do in talking about sex with your spouse, you think you are alone in your fantasies or desires—so it becomes routine, stale, or nonexistent. You are not alone, and the one thing that could be holding your sex life at arm's length is you.

These barriers will not be easy to tear down. By being aware of them, you can commit to your spouse that you both will work at not allowing them to keep you from the great sex you could be having. So, take a moment to identify which ones may be holding you back.

Next, PSST is an acronym that in this discussion stands for Prayer, Savor, Sensitive, and Timing. This is an easy way to remember the main points when it comes to having an exciting and deeper sex life in your marriage.

PRAYER

Like anything that deals with a faith in God, it begins with prayer. A person can't have a relationship with someone else without constant communication. So, to have a relationship with

God, you have to begin by talking to Him. Ask Him what He wants for your life, not what you want.

Now, with that said, He is the creator of sex, so why wouldn't God want your sex life to be amazing? Like I said earlier, I believe that's why people call His name in the middle of an orgasm—it's a way of praise to God during one of the most intense, intimate, and extreme feelings experienced on this planet.

I found from experience that my sex life became more amazing as my wife and I began to pray for it to be amazing. We began to pray that we would be into the same things in the bedroom, that we would find each other attractive and find all other men and women repulsive. This last part might seem a bit extreme; however, there are some really beautiful people in the world, and the last thing you need in your marriage are beautiful people turning your eye away from your spouse.

A final thought on praying for great sex in your marriage is that by opening that door to pray together, it's another level of intimacy that brings you closer together.

How about now? Pray together or on your own for God to show you ways to make sex *awesome*.

SAVOR

Sometimes, the main thing that can ruin sex in marriage is how fast it happens. There's just enough foreplay or none at all to get warmed up. Once it's over with, usually the guy is satisfied and the woman is left wanting more.

There's so much to enjoy, and if we slow down and take our time during sex, we can stop falling victim to being too busy, too lazy, or let sleep win over sex with our spouse. We need to savor the kisses. When was the last time you just made out with your wife on the couch or in the car after dinner? Savor those moments because the fact of the matter is that women are like crock pots and not microwaves. Men need to do all kinds of things, like acts of service for her, speak love in affirming her, and make her feel beautiful in order for her to be ready to have sex. A great place to start is with the firm kisses. At the beginning and end of each day and as often as you can during the day, giving more affection and investment can feed into her. The more you can savor a moment, a taste, or a touch, the closer you'll be to amazing sex.

Well, if you need to stop here and go really kiss your spouse, I understand.

SENSITIVE
(THIS IS MAINLY ADDRESSED TO THE MEN.)

If the truth be told, guys can be very agenda driven when it comes to sex. They are simple to turn on and simple to please. Not to mention that men have a seventy-two-hour rule that physically their bodies need a sexual release. All these things add up to fuel a lack of sensitivity when it comes to sex. Regardless of how romantic you are on any given day, there are two points of sensitivity you have to keep in mind in order to have amazing sex.

1. YOU HAVE TO BE TIME SENSITIVE.

To be time sensitive, you have to be aware of the time of day. Right before bed or after your wife has been dealt an emotional day with the kids, work, or just life in general is not a good time to make your move. If you make your move at a time when she's not ready, you face being turned down. If you pull off insensitivity over a long period of time, walls can be built up and anger can show up that makes sex less and less frequent and might lead to bitterness, a disconnection in your marriage, or, worse, an affair or a divorce.

2. BE SENSITIVE TO HER NEEDS.

I found that talking to my wife about what she likes during sex helps me to know how to please her. It helps me to understand what she needs from me to be in the mood and how she likes it. It's not about what I do minutes before sex that counts, but hours before sex.

Finding what turns your spouse on can only benefit you both. Ask her how she likes to be touched, find out what touches you already do that she enjoys or doesn't enjoy. It's not personal if you are doing something she doesn't like. You are educating yourself on what I believe is credit hours towards a master's degree in your spouse. Also, in the case for guys who "finish first," you can still help bring pleasure to your wife afterwards and give yourself some rest to build up stamina to possibly go again, which also benefits you both.

TIMING

Proper timing when you make your move for sex is vital. Keeping the lines of communication open about the best times for sex can help show you are being sensitive to each other's needs, and she will be aware of yours in return.

By heightening your awareness of what you can do to make sex great, you can create positive good patterns in your marriage. It usually takes three weeks for a behavior to become habit, so stick with it. You don't want to miss out on the best sex of your life.

SCRIMMAGE STARTERS

1. Has your sex life become a priority? Why or Why not?
2. What are you doing to improve your sex life?
3. How do you keep the fire going each and every day?

FINAL SCRIMMAGE STARTERS

1. What is one thing you learned from this workbook that has been helpful in your marriage?
2. What lesson(s) have you learned from other married couples?
3. What have you discovered/rediscovered in your marriage?
4. What areas do you pray about for your spouse?
5. If you found out tomorrow your child or spouse has a major illness, how do you think it would affect your marriage?
6. What goals have you and your spouse set for your marriage?

Signing Day
Your Team's Contract

MARRIAGE COMMITMENT (WIFE)

I, _____, promise to learn from other couples who have been married longer than I and apply what I learn and apply God's Word to my marriage. I promise to open up the vault and talk about everything with my husband. I will prayerfully look at myself in the hope that God will show me what I can do to improve my life in order to be the person He created me to be, so I don't lose my identity as a wife/mother but see it as an extension of who I really am in Christ, as a Proverbs 31 woman.

Signed: _____

MARRIAGE COMMITMENT (HUSBAND)

I, _____, promise to learn from other couples who have been married longer than I, and apply what I learn and apply God's Word to my marriage. I promise to open up the vault and talk about everything with my wife. I will prayerfully look at myself in the hope that God will show me what I can do to improve my life in order to be the person He created me to be, so I don't lose my identity as a husband/father but see it an extension of who I really am in Christ, as a 1 Timothy 3 man.

Signed: _____

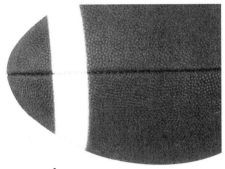

About The Marriage Playbook

The Marriage Playbook™ and Playbook Pep-Rally® are designed to be an energetic seminar, using music, videos, and activities to get couples focused and pumped up about their marriage. The Playbook Pep-Rally teaches God's design for marriage using sports themes. It's fun, nonthreatening, and always hilarious. Whether you're engaged, newlywed, or remarried, your marriage can begin a godly legacy. Find out more at http://themarriageplaybook.com.

WHAT CAN I EXPECT FROM A PLAYBOOK PEP-RALLY?

What should be in *your* playbook? This session will go over the basics of what you and your spouse need to have plans for in your marriage. Also, you will be introduced to ways to show love to your spouse and how to address the conflict of the five biggest areas that affect marriage and can break it apart: sex, kids, work, in-laws, and money.

NOT EVERYONE CAN *BE* THE QUARTERBACK

In this session the roles each spouse plays in marriage will be defined, along with the need for a coach.

THE 12TH MAN

This session gives ways to find accountability, and the importance of it, if your marriage is going to *win*.

SCRIMMAGES

This is a husband/wife breakout session, where all the women rally together to discover new ways to be better wives in their marriages while the men learn to lead and be the husbands they were meant to be.

PSST ... WE'RE TALKING ABOUT SEX!

This session tackles the sensitive subject of S-E-X and ways to make it great.

CONTRACT SIGNING

Focus your newfound energy for your team/marriage in a way that creates good habits in your marriage.

Find out more about a Marriage Playbook event coming to your community at http://themarriageplaybook.com.

ABOUT THE AUTHORS
Ace and Bethany McKay

The Marriage Playbook was created by Ace and Bethany McKay. Married thirteen years, both are FOCCUS-certified in premarital counseling and PAIRS-certified for helping husbands and wives communicate better.

Ace has been a professional broadcaster for eighteen years. He's also a columnist, counselor, husband, and father of two daughters. His journey into helping marriages came from watching his marriage to Bethany nearly end. After depression, affairs, and a shift of focus on career to a focus on God and on family, Ace and his wife have set up the Marriage Playbook to help couples see how they can plan their marriage one day at a time. They share how leaning on God can reconcile your relationship if you let Him reconcile your life.

Bethany is a gifted photographer, writer, wife, and mother. Her passion is to help women deal with depression bouts they may experience, along with making sure they don't let their identity become wrapped up in their kids or their husband. She has a passion to lift the veil on what a marriage should be.

Ace and Bethany are contributing writers for *New Man* and *Marriage Magazine*, in addition to e-zine articles, *Fort Wayne Family*, and radio shows across the country.